Sept 1/46.

Drs Stone & Kennedy

on Slave Wellen at

from May 1st to Sept 1st

$107 —

25

$132 —

Steven Kennedy, Carpenter

per S W Allen

1853

DAILY LIFE ON A

SOUTHERN PLANTATION

Collection of the New-York Historical Society

Paul Erickson

Lodestar Books
Dutton New York

CIP Data available.

First published in the United States in 1998 by
Lodestar Books, an affiliate of Dutton Children's Books,
a member of Penguin Putnam Inc.,
375 Hudson Street, New York, New York 10014

Originally published in Great Britain in 1997 by Heinemann Children's Reference,
an imprint of Heinemann Educational Publishers,
a division of Reed Educational and Professional Publishing Ltd.,
Halley Court, Jordan Hill, Oxford OX2 8EJ

Printed in Singapore
First American Edition
ISBN: 0-525-67547-7
10 9 8 7 6 5 4 3 2 1

Conceived and produced by Breslich & Foss Limited, London
Series Editor: Laura Wilson
Art Director: Nigel Osborne
Design: Paul Cooper
Photography: Miki Slingsby
Illustrations: Terry Gabbey
Map: Wendy Morris

CONTENTS

THE WORLD OF THE SOUTHERN PLANTATION

I n 1788, representatives of the 13 former British colonies met to draw up a constitution for the United States of America. By 1850, this new nation stretched from the Atlantic to the Pacific. At the same time, tensions between the Northern and Southern states were growing, and by 1861, civil war threatened the existence of the Union.

In the North, people made money by working small farms and operating factories. In the South, however, most of the money was made on large farms called plantations where crops such as cotton, rice, tobacco, and sugar were raised. Unlike workers in the Northern factories, who were free people earning wages, workers on the Southern plantations were African slaves.

Around the time that the Constitution was created, plantations in the South were becoming less profitable than before. Tobacco production was declining on the overworked soil of Virginia and Maryland, and prices for other Southern crops were dropping. Many people, in both the North and the South, believed that the plantation system—and with it, slavery—would die out.

In 1794, however, a Connecticut inventor named Eli Whitney patented the cotton gin, a machine that removed the seeds from the bolls (flowers) of the cotton plant. This made cotton a very profitable crop. So many people began to grow it that it was called king cotton. As the United States began to expand westward, new land became available that was perfect for growing cotton. The white planters who settled on this land brought their slaves with them because they could not grow large amounts of cotton without their labor. By 1850, the plantation system and the lifestyle that went with it had spread from the eastern coast of America all the way to Texas and Arkansas.

The Civil War, which lasted from 1861 to 1865, was the bloodiest conflict in American history. The eventual victory of the Northern states confirmed the end of slavery and paved the way for black people to take their rightful place in society as free men and women.

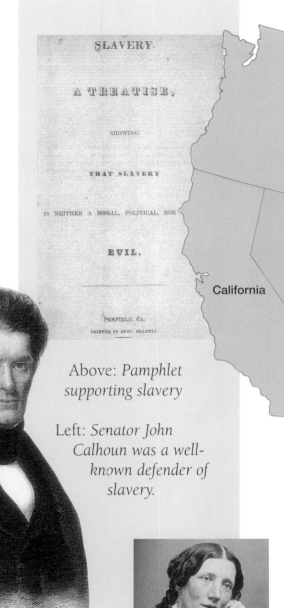

Above: *Pamphlet supporting slavery*

Left: *Senator John Calhoun was a well-known defender of slavery.*

Above right: *Harriet Beecher Stowe wrote the antislavery book* Uncle Tom's Cabin. *She argued that slavery was cruel and morally wrong. However, Southerners such as John Calhoun (above) argued that the slaves in the South were happier than the white factory workers in the North.*

The United States of America after the Compromise of 1850

Miles

0   250   500

0   250   500

Kilometers

Free State or Territory

Slave State or Territory

Territory Open to Slavery

The Debate about Slavery

Slavery had never been widespread in the North, and by 1810, it had been abolished in all the states north of Maryland and Delaware. Small farmers and workers in the North did not like the competition of slave labor in the South, and many Northerners read antislavery books such as *Uncle Tom's Cabin* and became abolitionists (people who wanted to abolish, or get rid of, slavery). Southerners continued to defend slavery, and their books and pamphlets were as popular in the South as the abolitionist ones were in the North. The debate about slavery became one of the most important issues in American politics.

For many years, new states joined the Union in pairs of one "free" and one "slave" state, to keep a balance between slave-owning and non-slave-owning states. But when California—a free state—was admitted to the Union on its own in 1850, this practice ended. At the same time, a new law was made to help Southerners reclaim slaves who had run away to the North, and two of the new territories in the West (Utah and New Mexico territory) were opened to slavery. These actions were known as the Compromise of 1850, and although they kept the Union together for the time being, they were not popular in either the North or the South.

The Slave Trade

I n colonial times (the seventeenth and eighteenth centuries), America was rich in natural resources such as good farmland, but it did not have the number of workers that were needed to grow crops. Although there were some poor Europeans who paid for their journey to America by their labor, the increasing workforce consisted mainly of African slaves. These slaves were thought to be the cheapest and most reliable source of labor possible, partly because their skin color set them apart from their masters and made escape more difficult for them than for European servants. Also, they did not die from "Old World" diseases such as measles, which had killed many Native Americans when they caught it from white people.

The work of African slaves helped to make America rich. Some slaves were first-rate craftsmen, and their help was badly needed because it was difficult to lure skilled European workers to America. The slaves also taught their owners many of the secrets of cotton and rice cultivation, without which they could not have made money from their farming.

Right: *A slave dealer's business card, wallet, and letter with details of a sale*

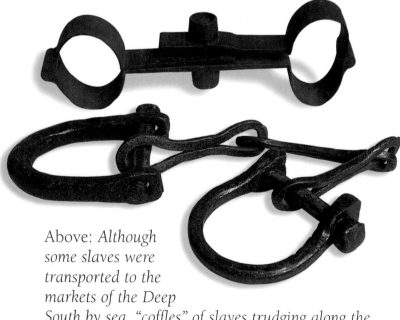

Above: *Although some slaves were transported to the markets of the Deep South by sea, "coffles" of slaves trudging along the road, bound by manacles and linked by chains, were a common sight. The slaves were followed by the trader on horseback with a whip in his hand and a gun at his hip.*

Slave Dealers

The importation of African slaves into the United States ended in 1808, but the children and grand-children of slaves in America were not given their freedom; they and their children were still slaves. Because there were no new slaves arriving from Africa, people who wanted slaves had to buy them in America, and a large market developed. As the number of plantations in the Upper South (Virginia, Maryland, Delaware, and North Carolina) declined and landowners in those areas no longer needed as many workers, they began to sell slaves to slave dealers. The dealers then sold the slaves to planters in the Deep South, where the number of plantations was rapidly growing.

Left: *A slave auction. Mothers and children were usually offered for sale together, but they would be separated if the buyer did not want to purchase all the members of the family. Very often, slaves who ran away from their masters did so because they wanted to be with a husband, wife, or child who had been sold to another master.*

Auctions

Slaves were usually sold at auctions, which were advertised on posters and flyers and in newspaper advertisements. A prime hand (a grown man in good health) cost as much as $2,000 in 1850 (about $30,000 today). Slaves with a particular skill, such as carpenters, mechanics, and blacksmiths, were very expensive.

Many masters would classify their slaves by how much work they could be expected to do. A full hand (grown man) was the most valuable. Under full hands came three-quarter hands (generally women and older slaves), half hands (teenagers), and quarter hands (young children), each capable of that fraction of the work of a full hand

Slave dealers could make large amounts of money: Each of the partners in the firm of Franklin & Armfield, one of the largest in the business, had made a profit of more than $500,000 (about $7,500,000 today) by the time he retired.

Left: *A notice advertising a slave auction. Among several slaves advertised for sale is "A Negro woman, accustomed to all kinds of housework. Is a good plain cook, and excellent dairy maid, washes and irons. She has four children, one a girl of about 13 years of age, another of seven, a boy about five, and an infant 11 months old. Two of the children will be sold with the mother, the others separately if it best suits the purchaser."*

THE FAMILIES

JOSHUA

CAMILLA

MR. & MRS. HENDERSON

WILLIE

The Hendersons

The year is 1853. Mr. William Henderson, now 56 years old, is the master of a cotton plantation in Louisiana. He was born into a family of South Carolina rice planters but did not inherit the family plantation because he was the youngest son. Instead, he was given some money to buy his own slaves and land. At the age of 22, he bought 2,000 acres of land and built his plantation. He is now worth about $210,000 (approximately

$3,100,00 today) in land, slaves, and property, and he has a yearly income of about $20,000 (about $300,000 today). Mr. Henderson rules over his plantation like a lord. He has more than 100 slaves, including 60 field hands, 10 house servants, two stable hands, three yard boys, and some elderly slaves and young children. He calls them his people.

Mr. Henderson's first wife died after bearing him one son, Joshua. Now in his early twenties, Joshua manages a sugar plantation owned by his mother's father. A few years after his first wife's death, Mr. Henderson married again. Mrs. Lavinia Henderson, now 32,

was just 17 when she married. As mistress of the plantation, she gives orders to the house slaves. She also looks after her 14-year-old daughter, Camilla, and her 8-year-old son, Willie.

ARNOLD BREWER

DADDY MAJOR

ROSENA

SCIPIO AND CICERO

Arnold Brewer

Arnold Brewer is Mr. Henderson's overseer. He runs the plantation and takes charge from May through mid-October while the Hendersons are on vacation. Mr. Henderson is lucky to have a good overseer like Mr. Brewer. The slaves know that although he makes them work hard, he is fairer than many overseers, who have well-deserved reputations for cruelty and drunkenness. In addition to Mr. Brewer's food and lodging, Mr. Henderson pays him $400 a year (about $6,000 today) plus a bonus for good harvests.

Daddy Major's Family

Daddy Major is a slave who was brought to Louisiana by Mr. Henderson as a teenager. He is now 49 years old. His wife, Rosena, is 45. She came to the plantation with Mr. Henderson's first wife. Although slave marriages are not legally binding because either husband or wife can be sold, Mr. Henderson likes his slaves to form long-lasting relationships because then they will make him richer by having children.

Daddy Major is the chief driver, one of the highest positions a plantation slave can hold. He and Mr. Brewer make sure that the field hands do their work properly. Rosena is the Hendersons' cook. She is in charge of the kitchen and takes orders only from Mrs. Henderson.

Daddy Major and Rosena have two sons. Cicero grew up with Joshua Henderson and is now his man-servant. Scipio serves as footman in the Big House. He is also the coachman and supervises the care of the carriage and the horses' harnesses.

THE PLANTATION

lthough few Southerners actually owned one, plantations were very important to the economy and way of life of the Southern states of America. Great statesmen of the South from Thomas Jefferson to Jefferson Davis were able to have careers in politics because their plantations, which were worked by slaves, earned a lot of money for them.

In the best farming areas, where most of the plantations were, over 50 percent of the population were slaves. However, most of the white people who lived in rural parts of the South were small farmers who owned only one or two slaves. Planters (men who owned more than 20 slaves) numbered fewer than 6.5 percent of the total Southern population, but they were very powerful. They controlled much of the South's money, and most of the white men in the region wanted to be like them, with large plantations, many slaves, and a lot of money.

Apart from a few luxuries, the plantation produced nearly everything that the master and slaves needed. Corn, beans, sweet potatoes, and collards were grown in its fields and gardens, and cattle and hogs were raised on its land. In the eighteenth century, well-equipped plantations even had workshops for blacksmiths, coopers (barrel makers), weavers, and tanners, but by the 1850s, these were beginning to disappear. Transportation was improving and slaves with specialized training were becoming much more expensive, so it was cheaper and simpler to buy factory goods from New England or Europe than to make them on the plantation.

Most important for any plantation were the fields where the cash crop (the crop that was sold for money) was grown. Rice and sugar were grown in the semitropical coastal regions of South Carolina and Louisiana, and tobacco and hemp (used for making rope) were popular crops in drier and colder regions like Kentucky and Tennessee. But, because it could be grown in so many different climates, cotton was by far the most common crop of the South.

Above: *A plan of Mr. Henderson's plantation. He has named it* Waverley, *after his favorite novel by Sir Walter Scott.*

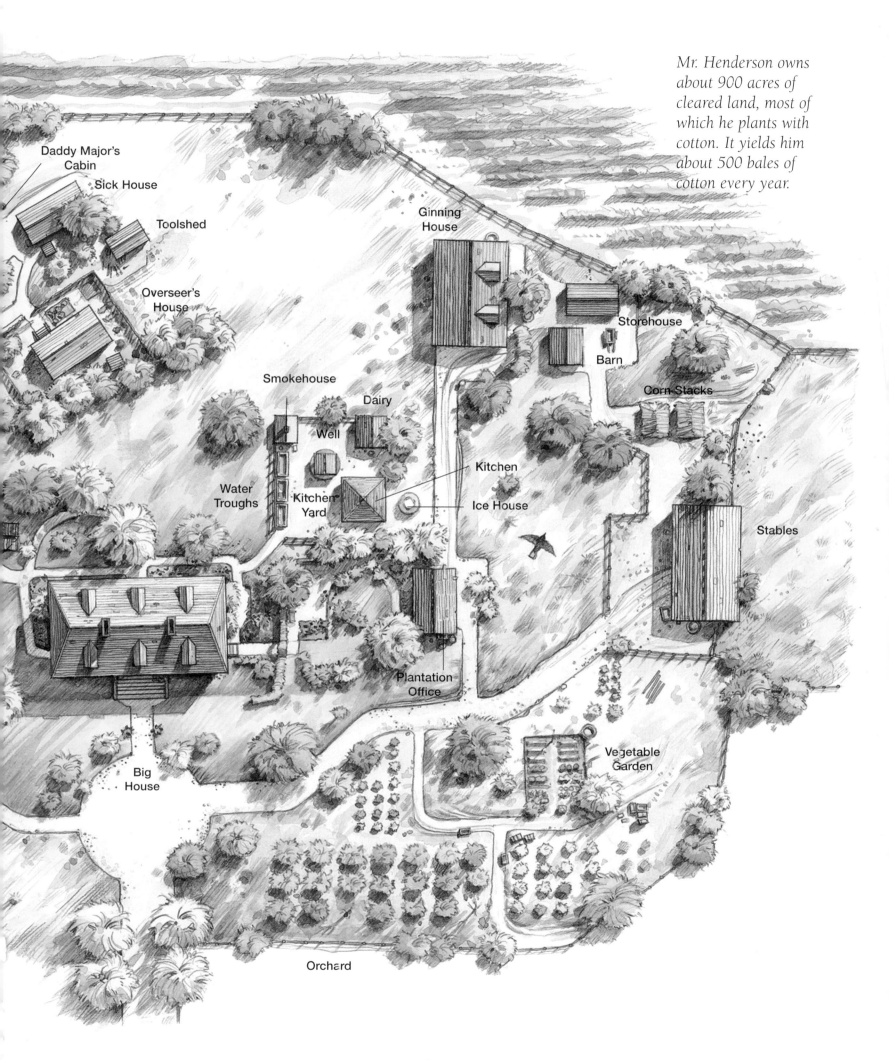

Daddy Major's Cabin

Sick House

Toolshed

Overseer's House

Ginning House

Storehouse

Barn

Corn Stacks

Smokehouse

Dairy

Well

Water Troughs

Kitchen Yard

Kitchen

Ice House

Stables

Plantation Office

Big House

Vegetable Garden

Orchard

Mr. Henderson owns about 900 acres of cleared land, most of which he plants with cotton. It yields him about 500 bales of cotton every year.

THE BIG HOUSE

T he Big House at Waverley was built between 1830 and 1831, at the time of Mr. Henderson's first marriage. Although it is not particularly large, this solid, dignified building is the most important one on the plantation, and a long driveway lined with oak trees makes it look very impressive. Bricks for the house were made from local clay, and trees on the site were cut down for lumber.

In front of the house is a large brick piazza shaded by a two-story colonnade. The colonnade not only makes the house look impressive but also shades the front windows from the hot afternoon sun. The columns are carved out of cypress boards, which have been carefully fitted together.

The decoration of the interior was expensive and took several years to complete. Slaves with specialized skills were hired from other planters to carve the woodwork and mold the fancy plaster ceilings. Imported marble, wallpaper, carpets, chandeliers, and furniture were brought up by boat from New Orleans.

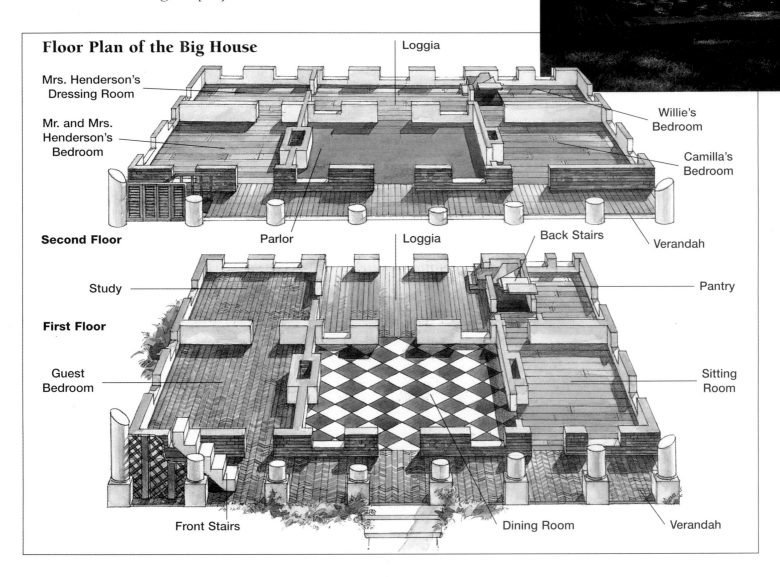

Floor Plan of the Big House

Loggia

Mrs. Henderson's Dressing Room

Mr. and Mrs. Henderson's Bedroom

Willie's Bedroom

Camilla's Bedroom

Second Floor

Parlor

Loggia

Back Stairs

Verandah

Study

Pantry

First Floor

Guest Bedroom

Sitting Room

Front Stairs

Dining Room

Verandah

Left: *The front of the house. On the left-hand side, behind the shutters, is the main staircase.*

Below: *The back of the house. The privies are carefully hidden behind the trees.*

The Design of the House

For the design of his house and plantation, William Henderson adopted the Classical Revival style, which was especially popular with planters. At the same time, to please his wife, he incorporated many features found in the French Creole houses of Louisiana's "sugar bowl" (the sugar-growing region in the southern part of the state). Throughout the house, tall doors and windows catch cooling breezes and funnel them inside. This is very important since the Hendersons have neither air-conditioning nor electric fans, and Louisiana has very hot, humid weather. As there is no running water in the house, the privies (toilets) have been built in the garden area at the back.

"*The oak-lined drive and the columns of the verandah lend an air of dignity and grace to the house. It is fortunate that the kitchen and yard, with their perpetual bustle and odor and noise, are screened from sight.*" Mrs. Henderson's diary

Above: *The main staircase leads from the piazza to the verandah on the second floor. The doors of the front rooms open onto the verandah. The back stairs, which are inside the house (see opposite), are used by the servants.*

Left: *The driveway is lined with oak trees, which are festooned with Spanish moss.*

13

Above: *This double pen or saddlebag cabin has two rooms with a central chimney. One family lives in each room.*

THE QUARTERS

Mr. Henderson, like many plantation owners, wants the slave quarters to look neat and tidy, with the cabins built in straight rows (*see page 10*). The slaves prefer their houses to be scattered about and facing different directions, perhaps because this was how villages had been built in Africa. Mr. Henderson did not like the way the first slave cabins were built at Waverley, so he constructed two rows of buildings. The street between the rows soon became the center of the slaves' social life. However, many slaves still live in cabins on the edge of the woods and fields, where they have more privacy and easy access to the paths and trails that crisscross the neighborhood.

The first slave cabins on the plantation were made of logs placed lengthwise on top of each other, with the gaps between them filled by mortar and mud. Now that milled lumber has become easier to obtain, new cabins are being built of boards, and the chimneys are made of brick.

"Daddy said that the master wanted to make the slaves build their houses in rows, but they wouldn't do it. They built them facing every which way. I don't know why they did that, but Daddy said it made the master furious." Scipio's reminiscences, as told to his daughter

Right: *Slaves made many of their own cooking implements. The trough, spoons, and fork are carved out of wood. The small round bowls are made from gourds. Only the iron pot is not homemade.*

14

Cabins

Some slave cabins are of single pen construction—one room with a loft. Others are double pen—two rooms flanking a central chimney (*see facing page*), or they consist of two single pens with a roofed but otherwise open area called a dog trot between them. In any case, the cabin floor is usually beaten earth, since well-seasoned floorboards are expensive and hard to produce. Typical slave cabins have one small, glassless window with a wooden shutter, which is really designed to let in fresh air rather than light. Doors are made of wood and have wooden hinges.

Because Daddy Major is the head driver, his cabin is of better quality than those of most of the other slaves, and it also stands in a prominent position, at the head of the street. In order to allow some privacy for himself and Rosena, he has constructed cloth partitions to separate a sleeping area from the living area. Their bed is made of raised wooden slats with a mattress of corn husks on top.

Above: *Daddy Major and Rosena's cabin. They are lucky—not many slaves have a brick chimney and a wooden floor. Some of their furniture is homemade, but because Rosena is a house servant, she is sometimes given furniture and crockery that her mistress no longer wants.*

Right: *A double pen cabin on the slave street*

EARLY MORNING

At 5:00 A.M., the plantation bell rings out through the November morning. Sunrise is more than an hour away, but the slaves know that they must start work before light. Any slave remaining in the quarters after sunup will be punished. Daddy Major walks from cabin to cabin, pounding on doors to wake the heavy sleepers. His job is to make sure that all the slaves are ready for work. Mr. Brewer, the overseer, has told him to whip anyone who is late, a task he hates.

The slaves throw on their clothing (*see below*), eat a quick breakfast of cornmeal mush, and pack a bag with their midday meal. Mothers leave their babies and young children in the care of women who have become too old or sick for field work, and then they all set off for the overseer's house, where they assemble outside to receive their instructions for the day.

Meanwhile, Rosena wakes the slaves who are sleeping in the kitchen loft. With the help of one of the yard boys, she builds a fire in the enormous kitchen fireplace and begins to prepare the Hendersons' breakfast. Since the morning is chilly, the maids are sent to empty the grates and start new fires in the fireplaces of the main house. Then they gather in the kitchen to eat breakfast and wait for the Hendersons to awake and give them their orders for the day.

The Overseer

Arnold Brewer, the overseer, awakes at the same time as the slaves. He puts on a clean white shirt, blue pants, and leather boots with cloth uppers. A breakfast of biscuits and coffee, prepared by his personal servant, awaits him in the dining room of his four-room house. After eating, he throws on his woolen hat and coat and goes outside. He gives instructions to the field hands who have gathered in front of his house, and walks with them to the fields to oversee their work.

Above: *Slave clothing of the type worn by men and boys, made of homespun cotton*

Left: *The big plantation bell sets the rhythm for the slaves' daily life. This one was once a ship's bell.*

16

Above: *The overseer's shirt is cotton, his trousers are wool. His footwear has cloth uppers to protect his ankles from burrs.*

Left: *The overseer's dining room. Above the table is a punkah or shoo-fly. At mealtimes in the summer, a slave would slowly wave it by pulling on a cord, in order to keep away flies.*

Slaves' Clothes

Clothes are distributed to the slaves once a year, at Christmas, so by November they have become threadbare. The men wear coarse cotton shirts and woolen pants. To keep warm, they bundle up in woolen jackets and cloth caps. The women wear long woolen skirts and cotton blouses. For outside work, they put on woolen shawls. Both men and women wear leather shoes. The original soles have worn out by November, and the slaves have made new soles from wood. They line their shoes with rags or patches of moss to keep their feet warm. The children wear no shoes, regardless of the weather, and their only clothing is a long cotton shirt that reaches their knees. There are no bright colors in the weekday wardrobe. Everything is buff or gray, except for the women's bandanas, which are made of colored calico and worn bound around the head like a turban. Bright colors, especially red, are favorites, usually worn on Saturday nights and Sundays.

"You've never seen so much commotion as when the overseer rang the bell in the morning. Daddy was always the first out. I don't know how he did it."
Scipio's reminiscences

WAKING THE HENDERSONS

Mrs. Henderson rises at about 6:00 A.M. Her personal maid fetches hot water, soap, and towels so that she can wash her face and hands. The maid helps Mrs. Henderson do her hair and get dressed. Over her long underwear, she puts on a corset stiffened with whalebone, a cotton blouse, and a cotton print dress. She asks her maid to lace her corset tightly, because she is receiving visitors and wants to look as slender as possible. When she is ready, Mrs. Henderson goes downstairs to give the house servants their first tasks.

At about 6:30 A.M., Mr. Henderson calls for hot water and towels. After he washes his face and hands, his valet sets to work shaving him. After his shave, Mr. Henderson puts on his clothes over his red flannel long johns. While on the plantation, he wears a white linen shirt, woolen pants, a frock coat made of wool, and leather boots reaching almost to his knees. He ties a cravat around his neck. After a quick brush of his hair and a splash of cologne, he goes downstairs for breakfast.

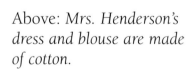

Above: *Mrs. Henderson's dress and blouse are made of cotton.*

Center: *Even a young girl like Camilla sleeps in a big four-poster bed. On the bedside table are a pitcher and basin for washing. Under the table is a chamber pot.*

Right: *People store their clothing and accessories in wardrobes like this one.*

Below: *Mr. Henderson's brush and comb set. The decanters are used to hold perfumes.*

The Children

The children are awakened by their old nurse, Maum Rachel, who now sleeps in the attic above their rooms. Young Willie is capable of dressing on his own, but he doesn't like soap and water, so it is only after Rachel scolds him sharply that he washes his hands and face. Camilla, on the other hand, is practicing her role as a young lady of fashion. She orders her maid, Betsy, to help arrange her hair and dress her. Today her clothes are quite simple, since no major social events are planned, but Camilla dreams of the Christmas season, with its many parties and balls, when she will be able to wear her best gowns and new satin shoes.

Left: *Favorite gowns and shoes are worn only on special occasions.*

THE KITCHEN

Behind the Big House, in the kitchen yard, stands the kitchen. The kitchen yard also contains a smokehouse (*see page 31*), a dairy, a well, woodpiles, and water troughs, so that the fuel and food that Rosena and her helpers need for cooking are nearby. Rosena is in charge of the kitchen. Even the mistress of the plantation, Mrs. Henderson, has little power here, and Mr. Henderson is content to let things be, as long as the food is good. He is seldom disappointed.

Rosena has been at work since before sunup. By 7:00 A.M., breakfast is being kept warm in a small oven in the pantry of the Big House, ready to be served. There are white flour biscuits, to be eaten with a meat gravy, which is thickened with lots of cornstarch and lard, but the centerpiece of the meal is grits, a Southern specialty made from cornmeal baked in a heavy iron pot covered with coals. The Hendersons drink coffee, which is brewed with chicory to improve the taste. When the Hendersons are seated at the table in the dining room, Scipio helps Old Ned, the butler, carry the food to them.

Above left: Supplies like rice, flour, beans, and coffee are stored in earthenware pots.

Center: Important ingredients in Rosena's cooking (from top): black-eyed peas, turnips, cornmeal, onions, rice, sweet potatoes, and squashes, with coffee beans and grinder.

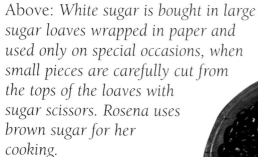

Above: White sugar is bought in large sugar loaves wrapped in paper and used only on special occasions, when small pieces are carefully cut from the tops of the loaves with sugar scissors. Rosena uses brown sugar for her cooking.

Left: *Inside the kitchen. Meat is cooked on a spit over the fire, and griddles for frying are hung from bars or hooks in the chimney. Bread is baked in a separate brick oven. Because it takes a whole day to heat the oven to the right temperature for baking, this is done only once a week.*

Below: *The kitchen building. In order to reduce the risk of fires and keep the smell of cooking at a distance, the kitchen is separate from the Big House.*

Open-Fire Cooking

Open-fire cooking is difficult. Rosena must be very strong to handle the heavy cast-iron pots and kettles. She must also be able to judge how hot the fire is at any given moment, and she needs to know the proper heights for pots over the fire, so that none of the food gets burned. Most cooking is done on the stone hearth in front of the fireplace. Rosena uses three-legged stands called trivets to support the pots over the fire while she piles hot coal on their lids, so that the food is heated from above and below. This is how she bakes the grits and biscuits.

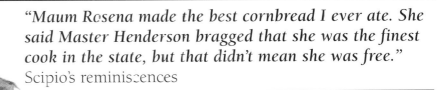

"Maum Rosena made the best cornbread I ever ate. She said Master Henderson bragged that she was the finest cook in the state, but that didn't mean she was free."
Scipio's reminiscences

21

Below: *A chimney brush helps clean flues and hearths.*

MORNING CHORES IN THE BIG HOUSE

After breakfast, Mrs. Henderson gives orders for the rest of the morning's work to the assembled house servants. Two maids are sent to clean the bedrooms. They open the windows and hang the quilts, mattresses, and pillows in the breeze to air them. They pour away the washing water in the basins and empty the chamber pots in the privies behind the house. After remaking the beds and sweeping the floors, they go to the parlor. Here they must beat the dust from the rugs, sweep the floor, and dust the mantelpiece before reporting back to the mistress.

Above: *Scipio and Old Ned work in the pantry cleaning the candlesticks and filling the oil lamps so that they will be ready when evening comes.*

Mrs. Henderson gives Rosena orders for dinner and sends her off to the kitchen. The scullery maid, who goes with her, sets to work washing the breakfast dishes. To do this, she heats a cauldron of water over a fire in the yard and pours it out into a trough. This is her sink, and homemade soap is her detergent. Another cauldron provides hot water for the laundry. Today the maid in charge of this chore faces a challenge. One of Miss Camilla's best white dresses needs to be washed, so she must first remove all the buttons and fancy trim. Then she will have to iron it carefully and sew all the buttons and trim back on.

Mrs. Henderson sends the yard boys to rake leaves and gather twigs on the lawns in front of the house. Scipio and Old Ned, the butler, unpack a shipment of wine and brandy, which will be stored in the shallow cellar beneath the pantry until it is needed.

Below: *Ice, which is cut into large blocks and packed in sawdust, comes from the Northern states and is stored in the ice-house when it arrives. These tongs are used for handling the ice blocks.*

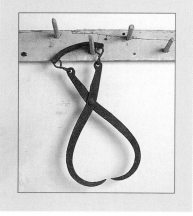

Right: *A washboard, tub, and irons are the laundry maid's basic equipment.*

Mr. and Mrs. Henderson

With the servants at their chores. Mrs. Henderson retires to her desk. As a plantation mistress, she is concerned with keeping a good diary and writing letters. This morning, she writes letters to several cousins and aunts describing her plans for next spring's garden. Then she writes notes inviting practically all the local gentry to a ball that she is planning for mid-December.

Meanwhile, Mr. Henderson has gone to his office. After writing a letter to his cotton broker in New Orleans, he turns to the most recent issues of *The Southern Agriculturist* or *The Southern Cultivator*. Like many planters, he tries to stay abreast of the latest developments in farming. As he is reading, the overseer arrives to give his morning report on the state of the cotton harvest, the weather, and the tasks of the field hands. Mr. Henderson makes a note of these things in the plantation ledger and then sets off for the stables to check on the condition of his horses. He takes good care of them, because he believes the old Southern proverb "A man is only as good as his horse."

"Saturday morning: light breeze, fair and cool. The overseer reported that the slaves in charge of ginning had broken a machine by leaving refuse in the hopper. Such carelessness must be deliberate." Mr. Henderson's plantation ledger

Below: A valet or ladies' maid often sleeps on a trundle bed. These low beds are stored underneath the large bed during the day, once their poles and canopy have been unscrewed.

THE CHILDREN'S DAY

On weekdays, Camilla and Willie Henderson go to school after breakfast. The schoolhouse is nearly two miles away, so they set out on ponies, accompanied by a slave who walks alongside them carrying their books. A few years earlier, Mr. Henderson and his planter neighbors built a small schoolhouse (*right*) and engaged a schoolmaster. Before that, they had depended on private tutors to educate their children.

Slave children do not go to school. In fact, several Southern states have laws against teaching slaves to read and write. The plantation owners remember all too well that, in the past, slave leaders like Gabriel Prosser, Nat Turner, and Denmark Vesey used their ability to read and write to help organize major rebellions.

Nevertheless, some slaves try to learn to read in secret, at times even paying freedmen or traveling black preachers money for lessons. Though their masters may not know it, almost every plantation has at least one slave who can read.

"When I was a boy, I heard a slave preacher speak at a funeral. When it was over, I talked to the preacher and gave him some money. Then I took reading lessons from that preacher. That was how I learned to read." Scipio's reminiscences

Left: *Boys play with toy coaches and horses, hoping that some day they will own real ones. Baseball is becoming popular in the United States at this time.*

Right: *Desk and chair. Children in wealthy households are sometimes educated by private tutors.*

Below: *School books and a slate. Young children practice writing and do sums on slates using special slate pencils, which can be erased afterward.*

Playtime

On Saturday afternoons, there is less of a gap between the children of masters and the children of slaves than on weekdays. They often play together, and a slave who is a childhood friend of a plantation owner's son or daughter often grows up to be their valet or maid. Willie runs off to find his friends, the yard boys, who have finished their raking. They know all the hidden trails in the woods, and he would like to join them in snaring a rabbit. Meanwhile, Camilla and her personal maid, Betsy, are braiding each other's hair and talking about boys.

School

School is meant to teach the rules of good conduct as well as reading, writing, and math. Students are required to learn passages by heart from the Bible and other classic texts. History lessons are about great heroes, and math covers basic arithmetic.

For the children of many planters, this is the extent of their formal education. Some girls spend an additional year in a finishing school in New Orleans or Natchez, studying music, drawing, French, and needlework. The important thing for a girl is to get married, and girls who have these refinements tend to find husbands more easily. Boys have only a slightly wider range of career options. They are expected to go into one of the professions that are considered appropriate for a Southern gentleman: the army, planting, or politics. So, after he finishes school, Willie might enroll in a military academy, help to manage a family plantation, or enter college with the hope of eventually studying law.

WORK IN THE COTTON FIELDS

Collection of the New-York Historical Society

Mr. Henderson's main crop is cotton, which has a long growing season and has to be cultivated almost all through the year. In March, the slaves plow drills (shallow furrows) in the cotton fields, sow the seeds, and then cover the seeds by hand. In May, the dirt is scraped away from the freshly grown cotton sprouts using mule-drawn plows, and the shoots are thinned out by chopping them with a hoe to create a stand. After this, the plow is used to shore up the roots with dirt. Throughout the summer and fall, the rows of growing cotton must be hoed constantly to eliminate weeds. Then, starting in September, the cotton is harvested. Because the cotton plants produce for several months after the first bloom, the harvest often continues into January, leaving only about one month of the year free from cotton cultivation. Even then there is a lot of work to be done—fences to repair, ditches to clean, and wood to cut.

Mr. Brewer, the overseer, keeps track of the cotton ginning and baling. The big gin is powered by four mules. The gin separates the cotton fiber from the small black seeds at the center of each boll. Once the seeds are removed, the pure cotton is thrown into the bin of the baler. Four mules hitched to a massive screw walk round and round in circles and the screw presses down the cotton until it is packed tightly. When a bale is at the right pressure, the screw emits a high-pitched shriek from the immense tension. Then the screw is released, and the bale is tied off. It is hauled off to storage by a team of mules. Bales of cotton typically weigh 400 pounds apiece!

Above: Work has finished for the day, and a line of slaves wait to have their bags of cotton weighed by the overseer.

Above: Blacksmith's forge

Left: Blacksmith's tools. Some plantations had slaves with particular trades, such as blacksmiths, coopers (barrel makers), and carpenters (see page 10).

Daddy Major

Field slaves always work in gangs, which are overseen by the drivers and the overseer. On this November morning, most of the slaves are picking cotton, for it is every master's dream to have the entire crop ready to sell by Christmas. As chief driver, Daddy Major oversees the cotton picking. He walks up and down the rows, urging on slow pickers and inspecting the work. Every field hand has a sack almost as big as he or she is to hold the cotton. Daddy Major often looks inside the bags to make sure that the harvested cotton is of good quality. The overseer sets the amount of cotton that each slave must gather by the day's end. The punishment for picking dirty cotton is 20 lashes of the overseer's whip, and for failing to meet the quota, it is 40 lashes. Daddy Major wants to make sure that his workers do a good job; in the eyes of the overseer, the driver is just as responsible for a botched job as the field hands.

"The overseer made my father whip the slaves who didn't work hard enough. Daddy hated the job, but he had to do it. So when the master wasn't looking, he would whip a fence post instead. Then the punished slave would rub berry juice on his back and walk off limping." Scipio's reminiscences

Above right: *The bolls of cotton grow on bushes that are up to 10 feet high.*

Right: *These stencils were used to label the bales of cotton. Mr. Henderson's bales are painted with his initials, W.H.*

Above: *The cotton is taken to the gin house in wagons covered with hemp nets.*

Tobacco and Rice

Although king cotton is the most widely grown crop in the Southern states, other crops are grown. States in the Upper South, such as Virginia, Maryland, Delaware, and North Carolina produce corn, hemp, and especially tobacco. In the lower Mississippi valley, sugar is the most important crop, and on the coasts of the Carolinas and Georgia, the low, damp land is perfect for growing rice.

Right: *A twist of tobacco and a pipe. Tobacco like this can be either smoked or chewed.*

SUGAR CULTIVATION

Joshua Henderson has learned the routines of sugar cultivation and now manages his grandfather's sugar plantation. This is not easy, because sugar requires the most complicated organization of labor, land, and machinery of any crop in the South.

Sugar seasons in the Deep South overlap, so the plantation is busy. As soon as the year's crops are harvested in the fall, the fields are prepared so that the next year's crop can be planted immediately. The slaves work in plow-and-harrow gangs, breaking the ground. In February, they plow furrows and plant the seed cane. Then comes a daily routine of hoeing, banking, and weeding that continues until the crop is left to mature in July. At the same time, some slaves are at work making sure that the crop gets enough water. Others cut wood for fires to boil the sugar syrup and to run the steam-powered machines, and build barrels for the finished sugar. In early October, the first cut of cane is matalayed, which means that it is laid out on the ground and covered with a layer of dirt. When the canes sprout, they will be used as next year's seed cane to grow the new crop. After this, the scramble to get in the crop begins: From October to December, slaves cut the cane, remove the leaves from the stalks, and transport them to the sugar house to be processed.

Above: *As the cane juice is heated, crystals of brown sugar begin to form. These are taken off the top with these ladles, paddles, and skimmers.*

Left: *A sugar house.*

The Sugar House

In the sugar house, the cane is crushed by massive rollers that are powered by steam engines. The sugar juice collects in vats and is heated until its water content evaporates, leaving behind the unrefined sugar. This is packed into wooden barrels to be shipped to market.

Working in the sugar house is dangerous and uncomfortable: Escaping steam or a broken roller can seriously injure the highly skilled slave engineers who repair the machinery, which means that their owners lose valuable and expensive workers. In addition, the simmering cane syrup gives off tremendous amounts of heat and steam, not to mention a smell that fills the entire plantation. The noise of the machinery often reaches deafening levels.

Above: *The furnace at one end of the sugar house heats up the sugar in the vats above it in order to boil off the water. When the crystals of sugar are skimmed off the top, brown molasses is left at the bottom of the pan.*

Above: *This painting shows slaves cutting cane, while smoke pours from the chimneys of a sugar house.*

Left: *Raw brown sugar. The dark patch at the bottom of the jar is molasses.*

Below: *A stalk of old-fashioned sugar cane with the leaves removed. Joshua Henderson grows cane like this.*

MIDDAY

Shortly after noon, Mr. Brewer rings the plantation bell to announce the midday break. The field hands stop work and make for the edges of the cotton field, where they open their bundles of food. Their lunch is made up of the traditional food of the South: corn and pork. There are slabs of cured bacon and cornbread to be washed down with water, which some of the slave boys have carried to the fields in buckets. The field hands eat quickly, because they must be back at work in half an hour. Normally, they get Saturday afternoons off, but during harvest time every minute counts, so today work will end at 4:00 P.M.

Rosena has prepared dinner for the Hendersons. They also eat corn and pork, in the form of cornbread and pork chops, but they have many other dishes, such as turtle soup, rice with crayfish and peppers, baked sweet potatoes, stewed okra, and apple and pecan pies. Cheeses and other dairy products are not served, because they are difficult to keep fresh in the hot weather of the Deep South, and there are also no raw fruits or vegetables, because they are thought to be hard to digest.

Mock Turtle Soup
Boil a leg of beef with fried carrots, onions, parsley, thyme, cloves, pepper, celery, and a piece of baked bread to make a good stock. After cleaning a calf's head with the skin on it, boil it for an hour by itself, then cut the meat into pieces and strain. When cold, take off the fat and boil the meat in the stock until tender. Add a little sherry and some Cayenne pepper.
From *Abby Day Broun's Receipt* [sic] *Book*

Right: *Typical Southern foods: biscuits, black-eyed peas, greens, ham, and cornbread.*

The Dining Room

The dining room at Waverley is on the first floor, where it remains relatively cool all year round. When the Hendersons gather for dinner, the mahogany table is set with china and glassware imported from England and France. A crumb cloth is spread over the marble floor. Dinner is not served in different courses as it is in Europe. Instead, Scipio helps Old Ned dish up whatever the family members want from the platters and bowls on the sideboards and in the serving pantry.

Mr. Henderson drinks whiskey and water with his meal, though if distinguished guests were present. he might have French wine served instead. Mrs. Henderson drinks barley water, which is believed to be healthful. As a special treat, the children have lemonade cooled with the last of the ice from the icehouse.

Despite the quantity of food, the meal is over in less than half an hour. As the plantation bell tolls and the field hands return to their tasks, Mrs. Henderson and the children rise and go their separate ways, leaving Mr. Henderson to smoke his after-dinner cigar in peace.

Above: *The slaves' midday meal, served on rough wooden plates, is cured bacon and cornbread. In the bowl is cornmeal mush, which is eaten for breakfast. It is simply cornmeal mixed with a little water.*

Above: *The table is set for dinner. In summer months, the chandelier and table ornaments are covered with gauze netting to keep off flies and dust.*

Left: *Hogs are slaughtered once a year, in January, and the smokehouse preserves their meat to last the rest of the year.*

31

A TRIP TO NEW ORLEANS

Once the cotton is baled and labeled, it is hauled by wagon down to the Mississippi River and loaded onto steamboats headed for New Orleans. Mr. Henderson often travels with it. The cotton bales are unloaded in New Orleans at the dock of the cotton broker, who makes an agreement with Mr. Henderson to buy his whole crop of cotton for a set price.

Mr. Henderson goes shopping while he is in town. The big times are coming—the Christmas season—when work will stop for a few days and the slaves will receive new clothing and other presents. Mr. Henderson buys ready-made shoes, stockings, caps, coats, and shawls, and some colored cloth and needles and thread so that the slave women can sew extra clothing for their families. He also needs more axes so that his slaves can clear a new field, and nails for repairs to the stables. These items used to be made on the plantation, but Mr. Henderson and other planters now find it cheaper to buy them in stores.

If planters cannot go to New Orleans, they order goods through the mail and have them delivered by steamboat. When they arrive, the goods are unloaded at the landing commissary (*see center*), where they are kept until the buyer comes to collect them. The commissary also serves as a general store.

"WANTED: one runaway, preferably ALIVE. Was a house-servant, literate and polished in character. He is known by a streak of white hair on the left side of his head. For information on the REWARD for his apprehension, inquire at the office of the publisher."
From a New Orleans newspaper

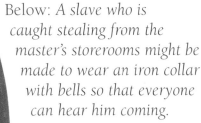

Above left: *A shipping certificate for goods ordered by a planter.*

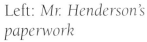

Left: *Mr. Henderson's paperwork*

Below: *A slave who is caught stealing from the master's storerooms might be made to wear an iron collar with bells so that everyone can hear him coming.*

Below: *Paddyrollers checking slaves' passes*

SLAVE DISCIPLINE

Although many masters think that slavery is natural, the slaves themselves hate it, and they find many ways to resist their master's authority. Some neglect their work or do it badly, and many masters accept that their slaves will be lazy unless they are forced to work faster. For example, if field slaves do not pick enough cotton, they are whipped (*see page 27*). House slaves are also whipped, even for a small offense such as serving a burned biscuit at a meal.

Some slaves run away from their masters, and Southern newspapers are filled with advertisements offering rewards for their return. Besides the professional bounty hunters who make money from catching runaway slaves, there are also patrols of men that the slaves call paddyrollers. Their job is to question any slaves they find off their home plantations and, if necessary, return them to their masters. If the slave has to run an errand off the plantation, his master writes him a pass to show to the paddyrollers, so that they will not suspect him of trying to escape.

Below: *Slaves who are hired out by their masters to work for large companies are given passes on printed forms.*

NEW ORLEANS GAS WORKS,..................186

№..........

The City Police will pass the slave boy.................-..................

33

LEISURE TIME

Country life moves at a leisurely pace. Mrs. Henderson sometimes supervises the gardening, arranging azaleas, rhododendrons, and other shrubs into a network of formal gardens on the south side of the Big House. Mr. Henderson enjoys riding around the plantation or hunting for foxes and wild turkeys in the woods and fields. While they are very proud of Waverley, the Hendersons look forward to occasional trips to New Orleans or Natchez, where they go to horse races, plays, operas, and balls, and meet their friends. To keep up some social life while they are at Waverley, the Hendersons frequently entertain visitors from neighboring plantations in the parlor of the Big House, or they go visiting themselves.

"Life passes so slowly out here in the country. But soon it will be Christmas, and there will be fancy balls and visiting and delicious foods. I hope Daddy will buy me some new dancing shoes when he's in New Orleans next, for it would not do to be seen wearing last year's."
Camilla Henderson's diary

Tea in the Sitting Room

This afternoon Mrs. Wilson, the wife of a neighboring planter, joins Mrs. Henderson for tea. Mrs. Wilson tells Mrs. Henderson that she is looking forward to next summer's vacation. To avoid the sickly season between June and October, when people are most likely to catch malaria and yellow fever because of the mosquitoes and the warm, wet weather, Mrs. Wilson and her husband usually go to Newport, Rhode Island. However, their Northern friends have recently begun to say that they disagree with slavery, which is embarrassing for the Wilsons, so they have found a resort in the South, instead, at Hot Springs, Arkansas.

The ladies also discuss Mrs. Henderson's stepson, Joshua. Mrs. Henderson hopes that he will marry the daughter of a rich planter, which would increase his wealth and land. Mrs. Wilson slyly mentions that Mrs. Henderson's daughter Camilla is coming of age (she is 14!) and that, although her son James is only 22, he already has land of his own. Mrs. Henderson is pleased to talk about this subject, because she thinks that James Wilson would make an excellent husband for Camilla.

Above: *Camilla's dancing shoes*

Above center: *The table in the sitting room is set for tea.*

Above: *Mr. Henderson allows his slaves to grow cotton to sell, but they have to grow brown cotton, because he is afraid that they might steal his white cotton to add to theirs when they sell it.*

The Slaves' Leisure Time

The slaves have little free time, especially in the harvest season when they have to work extra hours in the fields. Many of them also have vegetable gardens of their own to tend. To add to their weekly food ration of corn and bacon, they go fishing in the river and hunt in the woods. Skilled carpenters build everything from furniture to canoes and sell them at market, and some slaves grow cotton in their garden plots to sell, while others raise chickens (*see above*). They often avoid telling their master about this because he might demand some of the money they make.

House servants cannot do these things, as they have to be on call at every moment. However, they do sometimes take advantage of their positions to steal food from their master's table and storerooms. They are also in a better position to learn to read and write, and they can eavesdrop on the master's conversations. Any news of slavery disputes, runaways, slave rebellions, and emancipation (giving slaves their freedom) comes to the quarters through the house servants.

Above: *"Piano babies" were popular ornaments in Southern homes at this time. They were made of bisque and hand painted.*

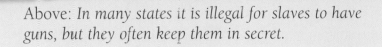

Above: *In many states it is illegal for slaves to have guns, but they often keep them in secret.*

DOCTORS AND DEATH

B y the 1850s, some branches of medicine, such as surgery, are quite advanced. Anesthesia has been discovered, so patients can be put to sleep during operations, but people still have not realized that the spread of germs causes disease. There is a great variety of doctors, from dealers in patent medicines, which probably do not do the patient much good, to mystic healers, and each one claims that his particular method of treatment is the best.

Left: *Rainwater from the cistern is often used for cooking and bathing, but this can become contaminated by animal and human waste, which causes diseases like cholera.*

Doctoring on the plantation is a mixture of common sense and local superstition. Mr. and Mrs. Henderson, like most planters and their wives, know the basics of simple surgery and midwifery from home medical books such as Gunn's *Domestic Medicine.* Country doctors can also be called upon in an emergency. Some slaves also have a knowledge of medicine, particularly of medicinal herbs. For example, the slave doctors of the Carolinas discovered that an infusion of dogwood bark could be a remedy for malaria.

Above: *Most wealthy plantations have a hospital or sick house for the slaves. Mosquito netting protects the patients' beds.*

Causes of Disease
Disease affects slave and master alike. During the summers, the fields and swamps of the Deep South become breeding grounds for mosquitoes, which give people malaria when they bite. Deadly diseases like yellow fever thrive in the warm, wet weather, and cholera is spread by infected drinking water. In these circumstances, slave doctors frequently treat their masters, and masters do the same for their slaves, sometimes paying professional doctors to treat them.

Left: *Babies and young children often died in the nineteenth century. Many parents have a painting like this done as a memorial to their child.*

"*Paid to Dr. Templeton, 32 dollars & 50 cents. Moses, Joe, and Old Tom took sick with fever Monday last and had to be bled. They are good workers, worth even more now that the harvest is coming in.*" Mr. Henderson's plantation account book

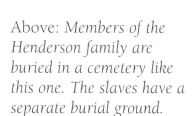

Above: *Members of the Henderson family are buried in a cemetery like this one. The slaves have a separate burial ground.*

Left: *A doctor's bill for the treatment of slaves, dated September 1846*

Below left: *Mrs. Henderson's medicine chest*

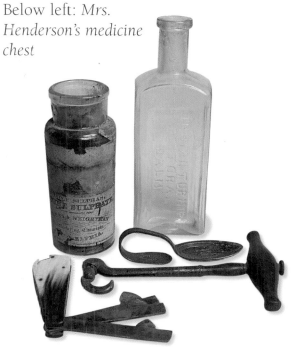

Death

When a member of a planter's family dies, a messenger is sent to tell the neighboring planters, and an obituary is printed in the newspaper. If there is a church nearby, a formal funeral is held. If not, the person is buried on the grounds of their plantation.

When a slave dies, a slave preacher usually holds a ceremony that the master attends. If the dead slave was with the family for a long time, the family mourns as if one of their relatives had died. Slave burials are carried out at night, in a graveyard for slaves only. African traditions are often observed. The mourners crowd around the coffin to stop the dead person's soul from escaping, and when the burial is finished, they throw pieces of clay pots on the grave (*see page 43*).

Above: *Medical instruments (clockwise from left): Quinine is used to treat malaria; a bottle for storing homemade medicine; a spoon for taking medicine; a tooth extractor; and fleams or bleeders, which were used to pierce the skin and make the blood flow out. This was thought to be a good remedy for fever.*

EVENING

By 6:00 P.M., Rosena has the Hendersons' supper ready. There is a big ham, fresh from the smokehouse, served with stewed apples. For side dishes, there are stewed turnips, collard greens, and rice. Scipio and Old Ned carry the food to the dining room just as Mr. Henderson is sitting down in his chair at the end of the table. Mr. Henderson pours his usual glass of whiskey and pronounces a toast to the harvest.

After the Hendersons have left the dining room, Scipio and a kitchen maid clear away the dishes. Only then can the house servants go out to the kitchen and eat their suppers with Rosena and Daddy Major.

Above: *Curling tongs and perfume help Mrs. Henderson prepare herself for supper.*

Evening in the Parlor

After supper, the Hendersons retire to the parlor. A maid tends the fire, lights the lamps, and brings them their favorite reading material. Like many planters, Mr. Henderson enjoys the novels of Sir Walter Scott. He likes reading about the knights in Scott's books, and often imagines that he is a lord in that romantic world and that Waverley is his kingdom. Mrs. Henderson glances through *Godey's Lady's Book* in search of fashion tips, and then reads the latest issue of the *Southern Literary Messenger.*

Camilla has been learning to play the piano. She cannot play the music of Mozart or Beethoven yet, but she can play the hymns of Lowell Mason and the latest hit songs of Stephen Foster, which pleases her parents. Tiring of this, she joins Willie in rearranging the Hendersons' collection of porcelain figures. "Do be careful!" says their mother.

Right: *The* Southern Literary Messenger *was a popular newspaper.*

Above: *Some of the Hendersons' most expensive furniture is in their parlor, including an astral lamp on the center table. Like the other lamps in the Big House, it burns whale oil.*

"Steal away, steal away,
Steal away to Jesus.
Steal away, steal away home,
I hain't got long to stay here."
Negro spiritual

Evening in the Quarters

At 4:00 P.M., the bell rings, ending field work. The slaves walk back to the ginning mill with their sacks of cotton, singing "Steal Away to Jesus." This means that, as it is Saturday, there will be a meeting in the woods that night.

Daddy Major reports the results of the day to the overseer, and the slaves form a line to have their cotton weighed on the scale in the barn. Then they go to the front of the Big House to receive their weekly supply of food. Mr. Henderson calls out the name of the head of each household, and he comes forward to get the food from Daddy Major, who measures out one peck of cornmeal and four pounds of salt pork for each adult, and half that amount for children.

Supper in the quarters means yet more cornmeal and salt pork. On Saturdays, however, the women try to prepare something special such as hoppin' john (a dish of rice and beans). There might be possum and raccoon that have been trapped in the woods (*see trap above*), fish caught from a nearby stream, or collard greens and squashes (*see insets above*) grown in the slaves' gardens. Daddy Major is lucky to be married to Rosena, the cook, because his meals are the leftovers from the Big House.

BEDTIME

A little after 8:00 P.M., Mr. Henderson steps out to talk for a moment with the overseer, who assures him that all is quiet in the quarters and that all the outbuildings, barns, and sheds are locked up tight for the night. Then Mr. Henderson retires to his room, where his valet helps him out of his clothes and into his nightshirt. His wife soon follows him, after making sure that the children are settled in their rooms and that Maum Rachel is close by in case they need something during the night.

Outside, the overseer takes a last look over the yard and locks the baling-room door by the light of his tin lantern. The quarters are dark, and everybody seems to be asleep. Satisfied that everything is safely locked up for the night, the overseer walks back to his cottage.

By 9:00 P.M., the Big House is silent, and the land outside is quiet too. This is unusual in the harvest season, when the slaves frequently work late into the night ginning and baling cotton by torchlight. Mr. Henderson snuffs out his candle and lies down to sleep, satisfied with the work of the day. Despite what the abolitionists say about slavery, he feels safe and happy–after all, the plantation and the slaves belong to him. How could it ever be different?

Below: *The maids carry the bathtub up to the family's bedrooms, so that they can bathe in front of the fire. The tub is filled with hot water brought from downstairs. The water in the pitcher is kept warm by the hot coals in the bucket underneath it.*

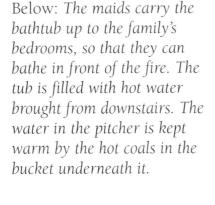

40

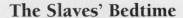

The Slaves' Bedtime

On every night except Saturday, Daddy Major, Rosena, and Scipio retire to their cabin after supper. They put out their single lamp *(left)*, which uses fat grease for fuel and has four wicks made from rushes, and then they settle down to sleep on their mattresses. But because there is no work on Sunday, Saturday night is special: The slaves have a meeting deep in the woods where they join slaves from other plantations and sing and dance until dawn. Mr. Brewer knows about these meetings, but he figures that his main concern is to protect Mr. Henderson's stores, so unless he discovers that things have been taken from the storerooms, he does not try to stop the slaves.

Left: *This commode is kept in the bedroom in case the Hendersons need to go to the toilet in the night. When the top is pulled down, it looks like a chest of drawers. The chamber pot can be removed by opening the lower drawer.*

Below: *In the morning, the servants empty the chamber pots in the privy behind the Big House.*

Above opposite: *Daddy Major and Rosena's bed is a mattress of corn husks.*

Center left: *Mr. and Mrs. Henderson's bedroom has a four-poster bed. Beds like these are often so high that steps are needed to get into them. Beside the bed is a washstand, with a basin, pitcher, and towel for washing.*

A SLAVE MEETING

Saturday night is the time that the slaves claim for themselves. They go into the woods, far away from the master's house, to meet slaves from neighboring plantations, sing, dance, and perhaps barbeque a pig over a bonfire. With the master and overseer safely asleep, they can talk freely and make music and dance in their own way. The slaves have a strong musical tradition, as their African ancestors used music and rhythmic dance instead of writing to tell their history.

The most common dance is called Pattin' Juba. Most of its music is provided by the stamp of the slaves' wooden-soled shoes on the ground. Settin' de Flo', another favorite, is more formal. The dancers face each other and bow while tapping the floor with their feet.

Slave storytelling is another art that has come from Africa. Uncle Remus tales such as *Brer Rabbit and the Briar Patch* are originally African stories. In all these stories, a weak but clever animal is threatened by a strong but foolish one. In the end, the clever animal (usually a rabbit) wins. Masters like Mr. Henderson are charmed by these tales, but they do not realize that they are meant to be the enemy and that the slave is the cunning rabbit. The slaves' favorite stories, however, are about Moses, who freed his people from slavery in Egypt. For them, the River Jordan in the Bible represents the Ohio River, which divides the South from the North, and the Northern free states are the "promised land" where they hope to live someday.

Above: *"Kitchen Ball at White Sulphur Springs, Virginia" by Christian Mayr, 1838. Slave dances, such as this one, were often fine occasions. The dancers here are wearing fancy clothing and fiddlers are playing.*

Left: *Banjo player. The banjo was originally an African instrument. It was brought to America by the slaves and popularized by white minstrels. This banjo looks as if it has come from a shop but many were homemade.*

Above: *"Plantation Burial" by John Antrobus, 1860. A slave funeral (see page 37).*

Sunday

Field hands do not have to work on Sundays, although house servants have to be on call all the time. The house servants often go to church with the Hendersons, but they, like the field hands, particularly look forward to hearing the sermons of the black preacher who sometimes comes to Waverley.

"Go down, Moses,
Way down in Egypt land,
Tell ole Pharaoh
Let my people go."
Negro spiritual.

Some plantation owners built churches for their slaves to attend.

Romance

Despite their long hours of work, slaves still find time for romance. At night, Scipio risks capture by the slave patrols *(see page 33)* to visit his girlfriend Jenny, who is a housemaid on another plantation. They would like to get married during the approaching "big times"—although slave marriages are not recognized by the law *(see page 9)*, slave weddings often take place with the master acting as the preacher. Scipio knows that his wedding will be difficult to arrange unless Mr. Henderson can be persuaded to buy Jenny, because most masters do not like their slaves to marry "off the plantation." Recently, Scipio and Jenny have been talking about escaping to the North, because they have heard stories of successful runaways living in Canada. Scipio has a good job for a slave, but he would gladly give it up if he could be a free man.

THE PLANTATION IN TIME

M r. Henderson bought the land for his plantation in 1819 and was forced to sell the plantation in 1874 because of his debts. Here are some of the events that took place in America before, during, and after this period.

1792 The world indigo market collapses. Indigo was an important cash crop of the South in the colonial period.

1794 Eli Whitney patents the cotton gin and makes short-staple cotton the South's new cash crop.

1800 In Virginia, Gabriel Prosser organizes the first major slave rebellion in U.S. history.

1803 In the Louisiana Purchase, the U. S. buys the lands between the Mississippi and the Rocky Mountains from France for $15,000,000, doubling the size of the nation.

1807 Engineer Robert Fulton demonstrates the first practical steamboat.

1819 The U.S. buys Florida from Spain.
Mr. Henderson buys 2,000 acres of land in Louisiana and begins to work his plantation, Waverley. He brings Daddy Major to Louisiana with him.

1820 Missouri and Maine are admitted to the Union together in the Missouri Compromise, keeping the balance of power between slave and free states (*see page 5*).

1822 Denmark Vesey, a self-educated black who had purchased his own freedom, lays plans for a massive slave revolt in South Carolina but is prevented from carrying them out when the white authorities hear about it.

1831 William Lloyd Garrison publishes the first edition of *The Liberator,* which gives details of the abolitionist cause. Nat Turner leads a slave revolt in Virginia, which leaves 51 white people dead.
The Big House at Waverley is completed. Mr. Henderson's first wife dies giving birth to their son, Joshua.

1832 *Godey's Lady's Book* begins publication. This was a popular magazine that introduced women to the latest fashions and literature.

1832-3 South Carolina refuses to obey the tariff laws (*see page 4*) and so denies the authority of the U.S. government.

A compromise tariff is passed to end the crisis .

1833 Great Britain frees the slaves in its colonies. £20,000,000 is paid to slaveholders in compensation.

1836 The Lone Star Republic (now Texas) becomes independent from Mexico.

1838 Mr. and Mrs. Henderson are married. Rosena comes to Waverley with Mrs. Henderson.

1843 Samuel Morse's electric telegraph operates between Washington and Baltimore.

1845 The Lone Star Republic enters the Union as the slave state of Texas.

1846 California becomes independent of Mexico as the Bear Flag Republic.

1848 The Free Soil Party is founded with the slogan, "Free Soil, Free Speech, Free Labor, and Free Men."
War with Mexico results in the Mexican cession of California and the Southwest to the U.S.

1850 The Compromise of 1850 admits California as a free state and passes the Fugitive Slave Law. This law made the U.S. government responsible for hunting down runaway slaves

and imposed large fines on anyone who helped them. Despite this, thousands of slaves escape to the North and Canada via the Underground Railroad, led by conductors like Harriet Tubman, herself an escaped slave.

1851 Stephen Foster writes the popular song *Old Folks at Home*.

1852 Harriet Beecher Stowe publishes *Uncle Tom's Cabin*, an antislavery novel.

1853 The U.S. acquires southern New Mexico and Arizona from Mexico by the Gadsden Purchase.

1857 In the Dred Scott Case, the Supreme Court decides that black people are not citizens, and that slaves cannot claim freedom by living in the North.

1859 Abolitionist John Brown seizes the U.S. Armory at Harpers Ferry, Virginia.

1860 Abraham Lincoln, a Republican from Illinois, is elected president.
South Carolina secedes from the Union in December.

1861 Emperor Alexander II of Russia emancipates the serfs.

1861-65 The American Civil War

1863 Lincoln's Emancipation Proclamation frees the slaves.

1863-64 Waverley is occupied by Union troops.

1865 Lincoln is assassinated.
The Thirteenth Amendment outlaws slavery everywhere in the U.S.

The Freedmen's Bureau is set up to help ex-slaves.
A white supremacist organization called the Ku Klux Klan is established in the South and begins to terrorize newly freed black men to keep them from voting.

1866 Congress passes the Civil Rights Act, which gives rights to the newly freed slaves. The Fourteenth Amendment makes these rights part of the Constitution.

1867 The First Reconstruction Act puts Southern states under military rule until Congress chooses to re-admit them to the Union. While these states will all be re-admitted by 1870, some federal troops will remain in the South until 1877.

1869 The Fifteenth Amendment guarantees black men the right to vote.
The first American transcontinental railroad is completed.
The first professional baseball team is organized, in Cincinnati.

1870 Hiram Revels, a minister from Mississippi, becomes the first black person to be elected to the U.S. Senate.

1874 Alexander Graham Bell demonstrates the telephone. Waverley is sold to pay off Henderson family debts.

1879 Thomas A. Edison demonstrates the electric light.

1884 Mark Twain publishes *The Adventures of Huckleberry Finn*.

1886 First manufacture of Coca-Cola.

1896 In the *Plessy v. Ferguson* case, the Supreme Court decides that separate but equal facilities for black and white people are constitutional. This decision upheld the Jim Crow laws for the segregation of black people adopted by the Southern states in the 1890s.

1926 Mr. Henderson's great-grandson William Henderson Harper buys Waverley and begins to restore the house and grounds.

1935-39 The Federal Writers Project records the recollections of ex-slaves living throughout the South. Scipio's daughter, Serena Potts, reports on her father's many memories of slave times at Waverley.

1947 Jackie Robinson becomes the first black player in major league baseball.

1954 In the *Brown v. Board of Education* case, the Supreme Court bans school segregation.

1964 The Civil Rights Act bans racial discrimination in public places and strengthens voting rights.

GLOSSARY

Abolition movement A late 18th- and early 19th-century movement to end slavery. Prominent American abolitionists included William Lloyd Garrison, editor of *The Liberator;* Harriet Beecher Stowe; and former slaves Frederick Douglass, Sojourner Truth, and Harriet Tubman, who made 19 journeys south to lead more than 300 of her people to freedom.

Boll The flower or opened seedpod of the cotton plant. Its downy strands of pure cotton fiber enclose the seeds.

Broker Factors, as they were commonly known in the South, bought crops such as cotton from planters and resold them on the national and international markets.

Calico Inexpensive cotton cloth printed with a figured pattern, common in both Europe and the Americas throughout the 19th century.

Cholera A short-lasting but often fatal disease caused by drinking water or eating food contaminated with certain bacteria. Symptoms include vomiting and stomach pains, followed by collapse from loss of water and salts.

Classical Revival Style Architectural style popular in Europe and America around 1770-1850, based loosely on ancient Greek and Roman models. Characterized by symmetry and many pillars and pediments, it was especially popular among planters who wanted to make their homes look impressive and dignified.

Coffle A train of men or animals chained or shackled and driven along together.

Colonnade An evenly spaced line of columns supporting a roof or ceiling. It is crowned by a decorative horizontal band, known as the entablature.

Commissary A commercial storehouse for goods and supplies, which often also served as a general store. Goods ordered by mail would be shipped to the local commissary, where they would by kept until the purchaser could collect them.

Corset A close-fitting woman's undergarment, usually stiffened with whalebone, extending from bust to hips, intended to maintain the wearer's upright posture and slender shape.

Creole A person descended from the French settlers who originally colonized Louisiana. After the United States purchased Louisiana from France in 1803, wealthy Creoles often intermarried with the new settlers, but they still retained many aspects of their French culture, particularly in southern Louisiana.

Cypress A tree common in warm climates, which flourishes even in swampy places. It was highly prized in the South because its straight trunk and resistance to rot made its lumber especially useful for building work.

Deep South The semitropical coastal states of Texas, Louisiana, Arkansas, Mississippi, Alabama, Florida, Georgia, and North and South Carolina.

Driver The immediate supervisor of a work gang of slaves, usually a slave himself, who was responsible for directing them, meeting goals established by the overseer, and punishing slackers.

Emancipation The freeing of slaves. Sometimes individual slaves would be emancipated by their owners. During the Civil War, in 1862, President Abraham Lincoln issued the Emancipation Proclamation, which said that henceforth all slaves in the rebellious Southern states were free.

Finishing school A private school for girls teaching deportment, social skills, and cultural accomplishments such as music and needlework.

Gin A machine with metal teeth for removing seeds and debris from fiber. The cotton gin was patented by Connecticut inventor Eli Whitney in 1794.

Gourd A hard-rinded, inedible fruit, which grows in a variety of shapes and sizes. When hollowed out and carved, gourds were used as spoons, scoops, or containers for liquids.

Hand A worker on a farm or in a factory. A "full hand" was one capable of doing a full day's work, and a "half hand" was one capable of doing half that amount of work in the same amount of time.

Hemp A plant whose fiber is used for making twine, rope, and coarse cloth. It was widely grown as a cash crop, especially in Kentucky, Tennessee, Missouri, and Virginia.

Icehouse An outbuilding for storing ice, typically a large, cool underground room. In the days before modern refrigeration, large blocks of ice would be "harvested" in the winter on lakes and ponds in the North, packed in straw, and shipped down the Mississippi or along the Atlantic seaboard. One of the icehouses at Thomas Jefferson's Monticello could hold 60 wagonloads of ice.

Loggia A covered area forming part of a larger building, typically open on one or more sides. In the warm climate of the South, loggias served as open-air rooms or hallways.

Malaria A tropical disease spread by the bite of the anopheles mosquito. Symptoms include recurrent chills, fever, and general weakness. If it is not treated, malaria can be fatal.

Piazza An open covered portico or verandah, typically colonnaded, extending along one side of a house.

Plantation A large farm typically worked by slave labor where a single crop like rice, cotton, or sugarcane is grown for profit.

Planter A person who owns a plantation.

Possum The opossum; a small, tree-dwelling mammal common in the southeastern United States.

Quota The share of work to be completed by an individual worker. A typical day's quota of cotton for a full hand during harvest time was 200 lbs. Those not meeting their quotas were subjected to punishment, typically 40 lashes with the whip.

Spanish Moss A mossy plant that grows in long, grayish-green festoons on many trees in the Deep South.

Stand A standing growth of cotton or other crop plant, often with a small mound or ridge of earth piled about its base.

Territory In the terminology of the Constitution of the United States, a territory is a region with some local autonomy but not yet admitted to the Union as a full state.

Union The United States of America. In 1861, most of the slave-holding Southern states withdrew from the Union to form the Confederacy, thus setting off the Civil War, which is sometimes referred to as the War Between the States.

Upper South The cooler and more northern of the slave-holding states, including Missouri, Kentucky, Tennessee, Virginia, Maryland, and Delaware.

Yellow Fever An often fatal tropical disease spread by the bite of certain mosquitoes. Symptoms include fever, slow heartbeat, black vomit, and jaundice.

INDEX

PLACES TO VISIT

The following museums and historic sites have displays and re-creations of aspects of Southern plantation life:

BOOKER T. WASHINGTON NATIONAL MONUMENT
Route 1, P.O. Box 195, Hardy, Virginia 24101
Tel. 540/721-2094

BOONE HALL PLANTATION
P.O. Box 1554, Mt. Pleasant, South Carolina 29465
Tel. 803/884-4371

CARTER'S GROVE
Colonial Williamsburg Foundation, P.O. Box 1776, Williamsburg, Virginia 23187
Tel. 804/229-1000

DRAYTON HALL
3380 Ashley River Road, Charleston, South Carolina 29414
Tel. 803/766-0188

FLOREWOOD RIVER PLANTATION STATE PARK
Route 82, Box 680, Greenwood, Mississippi 38930
Tel. 601/455-3821

GAINESWOOD
805 Whitfield Street East, Demopolis, Alabama 36732
Tel. 205/289-4846

LOUISIANA STATE UNIVERSITY RURAL LIFE MUSEUM
4600 Essen Lane, Baton Rouge, Louisiana 70809
Tel. 504/765-2437

LOUISIANA'S "GREAT RIVER ROAD"
Plantations along the Mississippi River between New Orleans and Baton Rouge include Ashland (Belle Helene) (7497 Ashland Road, Darrow, Louisiana 70725, Tel. 504/473-1328); Destrehan (13034 River Road, P.O. Box 5, Destrehan, Louisiana 70047, Tel. 504/764-9315, 504/764-9345); Houmas House (40136 State Highway 942, Burnside, Darrow, Louisiana 70725, Tel. 504/473-7841); Madewood (4250 State Highway 308, Napoleonville, Louisiana 70390, Tel. 504/369-7151); Nottoway (State Highway 1, P.O. Box 160, White Castle, Louisiana 70788, Tel. 504/545-2730, 504/545-2409); Oak Alley (3645 State Highway 18, Vacherie, Louisiana 70090, Tel. 504/265-2151); San Francisco (State Highway 44, Drawer AX, Reserve, Louisiana 70084, Tel. 504/535-2341); and Tezcuco (3138 State Highway 44, Darrow, Louisiana 70725, Tel. 504/562-3929).

MAGNOLIA MOUND PLANTATION
2161 Nicholson Drive, Baton Rouge, Louisiana 70802
Tel. 504/343-4955

NATCHEZ NATIONAL HISTORICAL PARK
P.O. Box 1208, Natchez, Mississippi 39121
Tel. 601/442-7047

MELROSE PLANTATION
Route 119, Melrose, Louisiana 71452
Tel. 318/379-0055

MIDDLETON PLACE
Ashley River Road, Charleston, South Carolina 29414-7206
Tel. 803/556-6020, 800/782-3608

MONTICELLO
P.O. Box 316, Charlottesville, Virginia 22902
Tel. 804/295-8181

MOUNT VERNON
Mount Vernon Memorial Highway, Mount Vernon, Virginia 22121
Tel. 703/780-2000

ROSEDOWN PLANTATION AND GARDENS
21501 State Highway 10, St. Francisville, Louisiana 70775
Tel. 504/635-3332

ROSEMONT PLANTATION
State Highway 24 East, Woodville, Mississippi 39669
Tel. 601/888-6809

SHADOWS-ON-THE-TECHE
317 East Main Street, P.O. Box 9703, New Iberia, Louisiana 70562
Tel. 318/369-6446

STONE MOUNTAIN PARK
P.O. Box 778, Stone Mountain, Georgia 30086
Tel. 404/498-5600

WAVERLEY PLANTATION
Route 50, between Columbus and West Point, Mississippi 39773
Tel. 601/494-1399

WESTVILLE VILLAGE
P.O. Box 1850, Lumpkin, Georgia 31815
Tel. 912/838-6310

Acknowledgments

Paul Erickson and Breslich & Foss would like to thank Harvey Broussard, Pat Kahle, Charlene Pesson, and Darlene Tighe at Shadows-on-the-Teche; John Dutton, David Floyd, and David M. Nicolosi at the Louisiana State University Rural Life Museum; Barbara Doyle at Middleton Place; and the Rev. William Dearman, Bettye Malone, Kay Juechter, Linda Morgese, and John H. Erickson for their assistance in the preparation of the manuscript.

Picture Credits

Louisiana State University Rural Life Museum: p.5 bottom left, center left, center; p.7 bottom left and right; pp.14-17; p.18 center; pp.21 center, right; p.23 bottom left; p.24-27; p.28 bottom left, center; p.29; p.31 bottom right; p.32 bottom right; p.33; p.35 top center, top right, bottom; p.36 top left, center; p.37 top right, bottom left, bottom right; p.39 center right; p.40 top center; p.41 top left, bottom right; p.43 bottom right

North Carolina Museum of Art, Raleigh, purchased with funds from the State of North Carolina: Kitchen Ball at White Sulphur Springs, Virginia, 1838, by Christian Mayr, pp.42-43

Shadows-on-the-Teche: p.4 top left, top right; p.5 bottom left; p.6 bottom left and right; p.13 center, top, center and bottom right; p.18 top left; p.19 center, top, and bottom right; p.20 top left; p.22; p.23 bottom right; p.24 center, bottom right; p.28 top left; p.30 center; p.32 bottom left, center left; p.35 bottom left; p.36 bottom center; p.37 center; p.38; p.40 bottom left; p.41 center

The Schlesinger Library, Radcliffe College: photograph of Harriet Beecher Stowe, p.4

The Museums at Stony Brook, New York: "The Banjo Player" by W.S. Mount 1856, p.42

W. H. Wills Esq

To Medical attendance
Maison de Santé
107 days at 19
To Operations d